Essential COOKING SERIES

COMPREHENSIVE, STEP-BY-STEP COOKING

Stir-Fry

HINKLER
BOOKS

HINKLER
BOOKS

Essential Cooking Series: Stir-Fry
First published in 2009 by Hinkler Books Pty Ltd
45–55 Fairchild Street
Heatherton Victoria 3202 Australia
www.hinklerbooks.com

Disclaimer: The nutritional information listed under each recipe does not
include the nutrient content of garnishes or any accompaniments not listed
in specific quantitites in the ingredient list. The nutritional information for
each recipe is an estimate only, and may vary depending on the brand of
ingredients used, and due to natural biological variations in the composition
of natural foods such as meat, fish, fruit and vegetables. The nutritional
information was calculated by using Foodworks dietary analysis software
(Version 3, Xyris Software Pty Ltd, Highgate Hill, Queensland, Australia) based
on the Australian food composition tables and food manufacturers' data.
Where not specified, ingredients are always analysed as average or medium,
not small or large.

ISBN: 978 1 7418 5704 7

10 9 8 7 6 5 4 3
14 13 12 11 10

Printed and bound in China

Contents

An introduction to stir-fry

The wok is reputed to have come into being around 2000 years ago when the Chinese first learned to beat metal thinly. Its design, remarkable then, and even today, is considered to have produced the most versatile of all cooking utensils.

The wok even revolutionised Chinese cuisine, for previous to its introduction, meat, vegetables and cereals were stewed together in large three-legged cauldrons stood over an open fire. With the ability to heat the wok to a high heat, Chinese cooks soon discovered the flavour of seared meat strips and combined them with vegetables and sauces, creating the wonderful stir-fries and fried noodles dishes, fried rice and deep-fried spring rolls, to name just a few delights in a long list. One utensil transformed a whole cuisine.

CHOOSING A WOK

There are many woks from which to choose, from the traditional cast iron with rounded base, to stainless steel and enamel-lined with a rounded or flatter base. Electric woks and woks with non-stick surfaces are also available. But with all modern applications, the traditional cast iron woks without doubt give the best result. They heat more evenly and quickly than newer woks but they do need more care. Woks may have one long wooden handle or 2 curved handles placed each side, which can be metal or wood. It is best to look for a wok with wooden handles, as the metal handles get very hot. You may insulate the metal handles to a comfortable degree by winding a good layer of insulating tape around them.

Large and small woks are available but it is wise to buy the larger wok, for a little or a lot may be cooked in a larger wok.

CARING FOR A WOK

The modern woks available will come with manufacturers' instructions for care and cleaning according to materials used, so follow their instructions carefully.

Cleaning and care of cast iron woks
When new, the cast iron woks have a protective coating designed to prevent rusting during shipping and storage. This must be removed, and the wok washed and seasoned before you can cook in it.

1 Fill the wok with hot water and add 2 tablespoons of bicarbonate of soda. Place on the heat and boil for 15 minutes to soften the coating. Tip out the water and while the wok is still hot, scrub off the coating with a scourer; a plastic one is best – do not use metal. Wash the wok well with a mild detergent, not an abrasive powder, and dry well. The wok should never be scoured again.

2 To season the wok: heat the wok to dry it out after washing, then wipe all over the surface with wads of absorbent paper towels dipped in peanut oil. The paper will colour brown at first, but continue the process with clean paper and oil until there is no further colouration. Rinse the wok with warm water, dry well and oil the surface with a fresh wad of oiled paper. The wok is now cleaned, seasoned and ready for cooking.

Care after cooking

It is important to maintain your wok in good condition.

1 Soak the wok to remove any hard cooked pieces of food. Remember we cannot scour the food away as the surface of the wok will be scratched.

2 Wash thoroughly with hot water only, scrubbing with a dish mop or plastic brush, never with a metal scourer or powdered abrasive. Dry the wok thoroughly (placing over heat is a good way to be sure) then cover the inside of the wok with a thin coating of oil to prevent it from rusting. When storing, never place any metal objects in the wok: they may scratch the surface. If possible hang the wok by the handle.

COOKING IN A WOK

As the wok is designed to heat quickly to a high degree, it is important to have all ingredients prepared, measured out and lined up before heating the wok. The following steps will guide you.

1 Measure out all liquid ingredients and place in small bowls or cups. Mix or combine any sauce ingredients. Blend thickening agent, e.g. cornflour, if using and have ready.

2 Slice, chop or grate all meat, vegetables and flavouring ingredients.

3 Line up the prepared ingredients on a tray, in order of use from left to right. Place the tray to the right of the burner. Have needed utensils ready.

4 Place a large plate or bowl nearby to accommodate the cooked food being removed, which will later be returned to the wok.

How to stir-fry

Stir-frying is the technique mostly used in wok cookery. The food is tossed continuously to allow all pieces to come in contact with the hot metal of the wok for a few seconds at a time. The best utensil to use for this is a special wok spatula called a chan. It has a curved end which fits into the curve of the wok, allowing total contact. Slide it down the side of the wok and under the food, then flip or toss the food over, allowing the top pieces to fall to the hot base. You need to work quickly.

ADDING OIL: It is important to heat the wok first on high heat until very hot. Turn down the heat to moderately high and drizzle the oil around the inside wall. As the oil runs down to the base it will heat and also grease the sides of the wok.

ADDING MEAT STRIPS OR CUBES: Add only a portion of the meat at a time. Stir-fry, as explained above, until rosy brown and remove to a plate. Repeat with the next batch in the same manner. If needed add 1 or 2 teaspoons extra oil before adding the next batch of meat. If meat has been marinated, drain well before adding to prevent the meat stewing and toughening. Cooking the meat in small batches also prevents the meat from stewing, as the heat stays high. Overcrowding drops the temperature of the wok.

1   **ADDING VEGETABLES:** Add the firmer vegetables first, as they will need longer cooking (eg carrots, celery, bamboo shoots) followed by the softer vegetables such as broccoli, courgette (zucchini), capsicum (pepper), mangetout (snow peas) and lastly shredded greens, bok choy (pak choi) and cabbage. Return the meat to the wok and toss well to distribute evenly throughout.

2   **ADDING SAUCE AND THICKENING:** Push the food up the sides of the wok to form a well in the base. Pour the combined sauces and blended cornflour into the well and stir until it bubbles, then stir-fry until all the ingredients are coated with the sauce and are hot. Serve immediately.

Cutting vegetables and meat

SPRING ONIONS (GREEN ONIONS): may be cut straight across into rounds. For garnish they may be cut with the knife at an angle making a diagonal cut.

CARROTS: look attractive if cut diagonally. Carrots may be grooved down the long side in 3–4 places then sliced thinly. They will look like flowers when sliced.

ONIONS: Small round onions are cut into quarters or eighths to form wedges then the layers separated to look like petals. Cutting into strips: Cut the vegetables into 6 cm long pieces then slice lengthwise. Stack 4 slices then cut through the stack into 3 cm wide strips.

SLICING MEAT: For a tender result, meat must be sliced across the grain. Purchase the meat in a thick piece or 'nut', not a slice. To slice pork and beef fillet finely, place in the freezer for an hour or more until it begins to firm. The meat will not move under the blade of the knife, allowing straight, thin slices to be cut. Cut slices into thin strips if needed.

Deep-frying in the wok

The wok is perfect for deep-frying. Because of its shape, you achieve the same depth of oil with much less oil than a deep-fryer. A wide surface area means more food may be cooked at the one time.

1   Heat the wok on high heat, turn heat to medium-high and add enough oil to be 2.5 cm deep. Heat until a haze appears; it won't take long as the wok is already hot.

2   Place in the food, 4–5 pieces at a time, and cook until crisp and golden, turning once. Remove and drain on absorbent paper.

3   Turn off the heat and allow the oil to cool before removing.

WOK SAFETY: It is best to use a wok ring when deep-frying, to ensure the stability of the wok on the gas jet or hotplate. Never leave the wok unattended when heating oil; it may heat quicker than you anticipate. Don't forget the wok was designed to heat quickly.

Lamb stir-fry with noodles and capsicums

INGREDIENTS

4 tablespoons oyster sauce
1 tablespoon dark soy sauce
2 tablespoons clear honey
finely grated rind (zest) and
 juice of ¹/₂ lemon
250 g (8 oz) medium egg noodles,
 fresh or dried
2 tablespoons vegetable oil
450 g (14 oz) lamb fillets, sliced into
 1 cm (0.4 in) pieces
2 carrots, cut into ¹/₂ cm x 4 cm
(0.2 in x 1.6 in) sticks
1 red capsicum (pepper), cut into strips
1 yellow capsicum (pepper), cut into strips
200 g (7 oz) bok choy (pak choi), sliced
200 g (7 oz) bean sprouts
4 spring onions (green onions),
 cut into thin strips
serves 4

PREPARATION TIME
15 minutes

COOKING TIME
12 minutes

1　In a bowl, combine the oyster and soy sauces, honey, lemon rind and juice. Mix
well and set aside. Prepare the noodles according to the packet instructions.

2　Heat the wok until very hot. Add the oil and lamb and stir-fry for 5 minutes until
seared on all sides. Add the carrots and capsicums **(peppers)** and stir-fry for
4 minutes or until softened. Add the bok choy (pak choi), bean sprouts and
spring onions (green onions), and cook for a further 1 minute.

3　Reduce heat and add the noodles and the sauce mixture. Stir-fry for 2 minutes
or until everything is hot and the lamb is cooked through.

NUTRITIONAL VALUE PER SERVE	FAT 3.4 G	CARBOHYDRATE 12.9 G	PROTEIN 7.8 G

Beef with green peppercorns

INGREDIENTS

500 g (1 lb) piece of topside
  or rump steak
2 teaspoons vegetable oil
2 cloves garlic, crushed
1 fresh green chilli, chopped
1 tablespoon green peppercorns in
  brine, drained and lightly crushed
1 green capsicum (pepper), chopped
3 tablespoons fresh coriander (cilantro)
$^1/_3$ cup (90 ml, 3 fl oz) coconut milk
2 teaspoons Thai fish sauce
serves 4

PREPARATION TIME
10 minutes

COOKING TIME
10 minutes

1 Slice the steak into thin slices across the grain, then cut each slice
   in half. Heat oil in a wok over a high heat. Add garlic and chilli and
   cook for 1 minute. Add beef and peppercorns and stir-fry in
   2 batches for 3 minutes or until beef is browned.

2 Stir in capsicum (pepper), coriander (**cilantro**), coconut milk and
   fish sauce and cook for 2 minutes longer.

NUTRITIONAL VALUE PER SERVE	FAT 7 G	CARBOHYDRATE 1 G	PROTEIN 15.5 G

Honey beef with pineapple salsa

INGREDIENTS

1 tablespoon vegetable oil
2 tablespoons sesame seeds
2 cloves garlic, crushed
500 g (1 lb) lean beef strips
185 g (6 oz) mangetout (snow peas),
    trimmed
2 courgettes (zucchini), chopped
3 tablespoons honey
2 tablespoons soy sauce
1 tablespoon oyster sauce
steamed rice to serve

pineapple salsa
$1/2$ fresh pineapple, peeled, cored
    and diced
1 fresh red chilli, chopped
2 tablespoons brown sugar
2 tablespoons snipped fresh chives
2 tablespoons lime juice

serves 4

PREPARATION TIME
8 minutes

COOKING TIME
8 minutes

1 In a bowl, place the pineapple, chilli, sugar, chives and lime juice and toss to combine. Set aside.

2 Heat 2 teaspoons oil in a wok over a medium heat. Add sesame seeds and garlic and stir-fry for 2 minutes or until seeds are golden. Remove seed mixture from wok with a slotted spoon and set aside.

3 Add remaining oil to wok. Add half the beef and stir-fry for 2 minutes or until brown, remove. Stir-fry the remaining beef adding extra oil if needed.

4 Add mangetout (**snow peas**), **courgettes** (**zucchini**), combined honey, soy and oyster sauces and seed mixture. Stir-fry for 3 minutes or until sauce thickens. Remove to a platter. Serve with pineapple salsa and steamed rice.

NUTRITIONAL VALUE PER SERVE	FAT 4 G	CARBOHYDRATE 9.6 G	PROTEIN 8.8 G

Beef and broccoli curry

INGREDIENTS

1 tablespoon peanut oil
1 onion, chopped
2 cloves garlic, crushed
1 tablespoon finely grated fresh
  ginger
1 tablespoon red curry paste
500 g (1 lb) rump steak, trimmed and
  cut into thin strips
250 g (8 oz) broccoli, cut into small
  florets
1 red capsicum (pepper), chopped
1 tablespoon brown sugar
1 teaspoon finely grated lime rind
  (zest)
1¹/₂ cups (375 ml, 12 fl oz) coconut milk
1 tablespoon fish sauce
155 g (5 oz) unsalted peanuts, roasted
serves 4

PREPARATION TIME
15 minutes

COOKING TIME
14 minutes

1 Heat oil in a wok over a medium heat. Add onion, garlic and
ginger and stir-fry for 3 minutes or until onion is golden. Add curry
paste and stir-fry for 2 minutes or until fragrant. Increase heat to
high, add beef and stir-fry for 5 minutes or until brown.

2 Add broccoli and capsicum (pepper) and stir-fry for 3 minutes or
until vegetables are just tender. Stir in sugar, lime rind, coconut
milk and fish sauce and simmer for 5 minutes or until sauce is
heated. Scatter with peanuts and serve.

NUTRITIONAL VALUE PER SERVE	FAT **12.9** G	CARBOHYDRATE **3.5** G	PROTEIN **11.1** G

Red beef curry

INGREDIENTS

1 cup (250 ml, 8 fl oz) coconut cream
3 tablespoons Thai red curry paste
500 g (1 lb) round or blade steak,
  cubed
155 g (5 oz) aubergine (eggplant),
  diced
220 g (7^1/$_2$ oz) canned sliced bamboo
  shoots
6 kaffir lime leaves, crushed
1 tablespoon brown sugar
2 cups (500 ml, 16 fl oz) coconut milk
2 tablespoons Thai fish sauce
3 tablespoons fresh coriander (cilantro)
2 fresh red chillies, chopped
jasmine steamed rice to serve
serves 4

PREPARATION TIME
10 minutes

COOKING TIME
48 minutes

1 Place coconut cream in a wok and bring to the boil over a high
  heat. Boil until oil separates from coconut cream and it reduces
  and thickens slightly. Stir in curry paste and boil for 2 minutes or
  until fragrant.

2 Add beef, aubergine (eggplant), bamboo shoots, lime leaves,
  sugar, coconut milk and fish sauce. Cover and simmer for
  40–45 minutes or until beef is tender. Stir in coriander (cilantro)
  and chillies. Serve over jasmine steamed rice.

| NUTRITIONAL VALUE PER SERVE | FAT **11** G | CARBOHYDRATE **3.1** G | PROTEIN **7.3** G |

Silverbeet with sesame seeds

INGREDIENTS

750 g (1½ lb) fresh silverbeet (or
  spinach) stalks removed
1 tablespoon peanut oil
1 teaspoon sesame oil
3 cloves garlic, sliced
2 tablespoons sesame seeds
juice of ½ lemon
¼ teaspoon lemon rind (zest),
  finely grated
salt and black pepper
serves 6

PREPARATION TIME
**15 minutes, plus
3 minutes standing**

COOKING TIME
5 minutes

1 In a large bowl, place the silverbeet (or spinach), cover with
boiling water, and leave for 2–3 minutes. Drain, then refresh
under cold running water. Squeeze out any excess water, then
coarsely chop.

2 Heat the peanut and sesame oil in a wok or large, heavy-based
frying pan. Add the garlic and the sesame seeds and fry for
1–2 minutes, until the garlic has begun to brown and the seeds
have started to pop. Stir in the silverbeet (or spinach) and fry for
1–2 minutes, until heated through. Add the lemon juice, lemon
rind, salt and pepper and mix well. Place on a serving platter and
serve immediately.

NUTRITIONAL VALUE PER SERVE	FAT 4.5 G	CARBOHYDRATE 0.8 G	PROTEIN 2.9 G

Sweet potato and tofu curry

INGREDIENTS

1 tablespoon peanut oil

1 teaspoon chilli oil (optional)

315 g (10 oz) firm tofu, cut into
   1 cm thick slices

1$^1\!/_2$ cups (375 ml, 12 fl oz) coconut
   cream

1 cup (250 ml, 8 fl oz) vegetable stock

2 teaspoons Thai red curry paste

375 g (12 oz) orange sweet potato,
   cut into 2 cm cubes

2 teaspoons palm or brown sugar

1 tablespoon Thai fish sauce or light
   soy sauce

2 teaspoons lime juice

60 g (2 oz) fresh basil leaves

serves 4

PREPARATION TIME
15 minutes

COOKING TIME
30 minutes

1 Heat peanut oil and chilli oil, if using, in a wok over a medium heat. Add tofu
   in 2 batches and stir-fry until brown on all sides. Remove, drain on absorbent
   kitchen paper and set aside.

2 Wipe wok clean with kitchen paper, then add coconut cream and stock and
   bring to the boil. Stir in curry paste and cook for 3–4 minutes or until fragrant.
   Add sweet potato, cover and cook over a medium heat for 8–10 minutes or until
   sweet potato is almost cooked.

3 Stir in sugar, fish sauce and lime juice and cook for 3 minutes.

4 Return tofu to the wok and simmer 2 minutes to heat. Stir in basil leaves.

NUTRITIONAL VALUE PER SERVE	FAT **8.4** G	CARBOHYDRATE **5.6** G	PROTEIN **3.9** G

Stir-fried vegetables

INGREDIENTS

2 tablespoons vegetable or peanut oil

5 cm piece fresh root ginger, peeled
  and finely chopped

3 cloves garlic, finely chopped

2 tablespoons dry sherry

1 red capsicum (pepper), cut into
  2.5 cm squares

1 yellow capsicum (pepper), cut into
  2.5 cm squares

2 medium carrots, peeled and thinly
  sliced on the diagonal

350 g (11¹/₂ oz) broccoli, cut into small
  florets and stalks thinly sliced

300 g (10 oz) brown cap mushrooms,
  wiped and thickly sliced

2 tablespoons soy sauce

8 spring onions (green onions), cut into
  1 cm diagonal slices

serves 4

PREPARATION TIME
25 minutes

COOKING TIME
11 minutes

1 Prepare and cut all vegetables. Measure liquid ingredients and place in small bowls.
   Arrange all in order of inclusion.

2 Heat a large wok over a high heat for 1 minute. Add the oil and rotate the wok to
   coat the base and lower sides. Add the ginger and garlic and stir-fry for 30 seconds.
   Add the sherry and cook for a further 15 seconds. Add the capsicums (peppers) and
   carrots and continue to stir-fry for 5 minutes or until the vegetables start to soften.

3 Add the broccoli, mushrooms and soy sauce and stir-fry for 3 minutes or until all the
   vegetables are just tender. Add the spring onions (green onions) and stir-fry for
   1 minute. Serve immediately.

NUTRITIONAL VALUE PER SERVE	FAT 3.3 G	CARBOHYDRATE 2.4 G	PROTEIN 3.0 G

Pork stir-fry with mangetout

INGREDIENTS

500 g (1 lb) pork stir-fry strips
2 teaspoons cornflour
1 tablespoon rice wine or dry sherry
   (optional)
2 tablespoons soy sauce
2 tablespoons peanut oil
2 cloves garlic, crushed
1 cm piece ginger, chopped
1 small red chilli, deseeded and sliced
6 spring onions (green onions),
   cut into 3 cm pieces
180 g (6 oz) mangetout (snow peas),
   halved

sauce
2–3 tablespoons oyster sauce
1 teaspoon sugar
¹/₂ cup (125 ml, 4 fl oz) chicken stock
serves 4

PREPARATION TIME
15 minutes,
plus 10 minutes
marinating

COOKING TIME
10 minutes

1 In a bowl, combine the oyster sauce, sugar and chicken stock and set aside. In a
glass bowl, combine the pork with cornflour, rice wine and soy sauce. Marinate
for 10 minutes.

2 Heat the wok to very hot. Add 2 teaspoons of oil and half of the pork and stir-fry
for 2 minutes until cooked and browned. Remove. Add 2 teaspoons of oil and
remaining pork, cook as above and remove from wok.

3 Add garlic, ginger and chilli and more oil if needed and stir-fry for 1 minute.
Toss in spring onions (green onions) and mangetout (snow peas), and stir-fry
for 2 minutes. Return the pork and stir-fry to heat through. Pour in sauce and
toss well to combine. Pile into serving bowls and serve immediately.

NUTRITIONAL VALUE PER SERVE	FAT 4.6G	CARBOHYDRATE 3.7 G	PROTEIN 11.2 G

Pork and pumpkin stir-fry

INGREDIENTS

1 tablespoon vegetable oil
500 g (1 lb) lean pork strips
2 onions, cut into thin wedges,
  layers separated
2 tablespoons Thai red curry paste
500 g (1 lb) peeled butternut
  pumpkin, cut into 2 cm cubes
4 kaffir lime leaves, shredded
1 tablespoon palm or brown sugar
2 cups (500 ml, 16 fl oz) coconut milk
1 tablespoon Thai fish sauce
serves 4

PREPARATION TIME
10 minutes

COOKING TIME
12 minutes

1 Heat the wok on high heat. Add half the oil and pork strips and
stir-fry for 2 minutes or until browned. Remove. Add remaining oil
and pork and cook as above.

2 Add the onions and stir-fry until soft. Stir in the curry paste and
stir-fry for 1 minute.

3 Add the pumpkin, lime leaves, sugar, coconut milk and fish sauce.
Stir, bring to the boil and simmer for 3 minutes. Return the pork
to the wok and stir-fry for 2 minutes until heated through. Serve
immediately.

NUTRITIONAL VALUE PER SERVE   FAT **8.4** G   CARBOHYDRATE **4.4** G   PROTEIN **7.6** G

Balsamic pork stir-fry

INGREDIENTS

2 teaspoons olive oil
2 cloves garlic, crushed
500 g (1 lb) pork fillet, trimmed,
  cut into 1 cm thick slices
1 red capsicum (pepper), chopped
1 green capsicum (pepper), chopped
$^1/_2$ cup (125 ml, 4 fl oz) orange juice
4 tablespoons balsamic vinegar
freshly ground black pepper
125 g (4 oz) rocket or watercress
  leaves
steamed rice to serve
serves 4

1 Heat wok over a high heat. Add oil and garlic
   and stir-fry for 1 minute or until golden. Add
   pork and stir-fry for 3 minutes or until brown.
   Add capsicums (peppers), orange juice and
   vinegar and stir-fry for 3 minutes or until pork
   is cooked. Season to taste with black pepper.

2 Divide rocket or watercress between serving
   plates, then top with pork mixture. Serve
   immediately with steamed rice.

PREPARATION TIME
10 minutes

COOKING TIME
6 minutes

NUTRITIONAL VALUE PER SERVE	FAT **2.2** G	CARBOHYDRATE **1.9** G	PROTEIN **11.5** G

Lime-glazed chicken wings

INGREDIENTS

1 kg (2 lb, approximately 12) chicken
  wings, tips removed
4 tablespoons lime juice
1 tablespoon white-wine vinegar
2 tablespoons brown sugar
2 teaspoons soy sauce
2 tablespoons oil
4 spring onions (green onions),
  diagonally sliced
2 limes, thinly sliced
$^1/_2$ cup (125 ml, 4 fl oz) water
4 tablespoons white sugar
$^1/_2$ teaspoon white-wine vinegar
makes 12

1 Place chicken wings in a flat non-metal
container. In a bowl, combine lime juice,
vinegar, sugar and soy sauce. Pour over the
wings and turn to coat. Marinate for 30
minutes or longer.

2 Heat the wok and add oil. Remove wings
from marinade and stir-fry about 15 minutes
until brown and tender. Add spring onions
(green onions) and stir-fry 1 minute. Pour in
the marinade. Stir to coat and heat through.
Remove to a platter and keep hot.

3 Add the lime and water to the wok and simmer
2 minutes. Stir in the sugar and vinegar, and
cook until slices are coated with a thick syrup.
Arrange slices over the wings. Pour over
remaining syrup. Serve as finger food or as a
meal with rice and vegetables.

PREPARATION TIME
10 minutes,
plus 30 minutes
marinating

COOKING TIME
18 minutes

NUTRITIONAL VALUE PER SERVE   FAT **5.5** G   CARBOHYDRATE **6.2** G   PROTEIN **13.7** G

Garlic pepper chicken

INGREDIENTS

2 teaspoons vegetable oil
4 cloves garlic, crushed
1 teaspoon black peppercorns,
  crushed
4 chicken breast fillets, sliced
$^1/_2$ cup (125 ml, 4 fl oz) chicken stock
4 tablespoons dry white wine
1 tablespoon soy sauce
155 g (5 oz) young English spinach
  leaves
serves 4

PREPARATION TIME
5 minutes

COOKING TIME
8 minutes

1 Heat oil in a wok over a medium heat. Add garlic and black
peppercorns and stir-fry for 1 minute or until garlic is golden. Add
chicken and stir-fry for 3 minutes or until brown.

2 Stir in stock, wine and soy sauce. Bring to simmering point and
simmer for 4 minutes or until sauce reduces by half.

3 Arrange spinach leaves on serving plates and top with chicken
mixture. Serve immediately.

NUTRITIONAL VALUE PER SERVE	FAT **4.8** G	CARBOHYDRATE **1.9** G	PROTEIN **17** G

Samosas

INGREDIENTS

1 tablespoon vegetable oil
2 medium onions, finely
  chopped
1 clove garlic, crushed
2 teaspoons curry paste
$^1/_2$ teaspoon salt
1 tablespoon white vinegar
250 g (8 oz) chicken mince
$^1/_2$ cup (125 ml, 4 fl oz) water
2 teaspoons sweet chilli sauce
  (or jalapeño jelly)
2 tablespoons chopped
  coriander (cilantro)
1 packet spring roll wrappers
oil for deep frying
makes 30

1 Heat the wok, add oil and fry onions and garlic until soft. Stir in curry paste, salt and vinegar. Add chicken mince and stir-fry on high until it changes colour. Reduce the heat. Add the water, cover and cook about 6 minutes until most of the water is absorbed. Add sweet chilli sauce (or jalapeño jelly) and coriander (cilantro), stir to mix well. Remove to a plate to cool.

2 Cut 10 spring roll wrappers into 3 even pieces lengthwise. Place a teaspoon of filling at the end and fold the pastry over diagonally, forming a triangle. Fold again on the straight and continue to end of strip. Moisten the inside edge of the last fold with water and press gently to seal.

3 Heat clean wok. Add enough oil to be approximately 5 cm deep and heat. Add 3–4 samosas at a time and fry until golden. Remove to a tray lined with paper towels. Serve hot.

PREPARATION TIME
15 minutes

COOKING TIME
30 minutes

NUTRITIONAL VALUE PER SERVE	FAT **25.2** G	CARBOHYDRATE **12.6** G	PROTEIN **5.9** G

Stir-fry chicken with almonds and broccoli

INGREDIENTS

200 g (7 oz) broccoli florets
500 g (1 lb) chicken stir-fry pieces
3 teaspoons cornflour
$^1/_2$ teaspoon five-spice powder
$^1/_2$ teaspoon salt
oil for frying
150 g (5 oz) blanched almonds
1$^1/_2$ teaspoons finely chopped
   fresh ginger
1 clove garlic, crushed
2 tablespoons dry sherry
1 teaspoon sugar
1 tablespoon soy sauce
2 teaspoons water
2 teaspoons cornflour
boiled rice to serve
serves 4

1 Place broccoli florets in boiling water for 1 minute, then remove to a bowl of iced water, stand 5 minutes, drain and set aside. Place the chicken in a bowl and sprinkle with cornflour, five-spice powder and salt. Mix well and set aside.

2 Heat 2 tablespoons oil in the wok and fry the almonds until golden. Remove, drain and set aside. Add the ginger and garlic and stir-fry for 1 minute. Add the chicken in batches and stir-fry until the chicken is cooked.

3 Return all the chicken to the wok and add the sherry, sugar and soy sauce. Stir a little then add the combined water and cornflour. Stir-fry until the sauce thickens. Add the blanched broccoli and fried almonds and toss to heat through. Serve immediately with boiled rice.

PREPARATION TIME
15 minutes

COOKING TIME
10 minutes

NUTRITIONAL VALUE PER SERVE   FAT **9.7** G   CARBOHYDRATE **13.4** G   PROTEIN **10.4** G

Chicken salad with mint dressing

INGREDIENTS

1 teaspoon sesame oil
1 teaspoon chilli oil
1 stalk fresh lemongrass, finely chopped
315 g (10 oz) lean chicken mince
185 g (6 oz) water chestnuts, chopped
1 tablespoon soy sauce
1 red capsicum (pepper), thinly sliced
1 green capsicum (pepper), thinly sliced
60 g (2 oz) bean sprouts
45 g (1½ oz) shredded coconut, toasted
200 g (7 oz) assorted lettuce leaves
mint dressing
3 tablespoons chopped fresh mint
1 clove garlic, crushed
1 tablespoon brown sugar
4 tablespoons water
1 tablespoon fish sauce
1 tablespoon lime juice
serves 4

PREPARATION TIME
5 minutes

COOKING TIME
8 minutes

1 In a bowl, place the mint, garlic, sugar, water, fish sauce and lime juice and mix to combine. Set aside. Heat sesame and chilli oils in a wok over a medium heat. Add the lemongrass and stir-fry for 2 minutes or until golden. Add the chicken, water chestnuts and soy sauce and stir-fry for 5 minutes or until chicken is tender. Remove pan from heat and cool slightly.

2 In a bowl, place the chicken mixture, capsicums (peppers), bean sprouts and coconut and toss to combine. Place the lettuce leaves on a large platter and arrange the chicken mixture on top.

NUTRITIONAL VALUE PER SERVE   FAT **4.1** G   CARBOHYDRATE **3.9** G   PROTEIN **6.5** G

Pad Thai with pork and prawns

INGREDIENTS

250 g (8 oz) rice noodles
4 tablespoons peanut oil
2 cloves garlic, chopped
1 shallot, chopped
125 g (4 oz) pork fillet, cut into 5 mm
  thick strips
1 tablespoon Thai fish sauce
1 teaspoon sugar
juice of $\frac{1}{2}$ lime
1 tablespoon light soy sauce
1 tablespoon tomato sauce
200 g (7 oz) fresh bean sprouts
125 g (4 oz) cooked and peeled prawns
  (shrimps)
black pepper
60 g (2 oz) roasted salted peanuts, chopped
1 tablespoon chopped fresh coriander
  (cilantro)
1 lime, quartered, to serve

serves 4

PREPARATION TIME
20 minutes

COOKING TIME
15 minutes

1 Prepare the rice noodles according to the packet instructions, rinse and drain well. Heat a wok. Add the oil, garlic, shallot and pork and stir-fry for 3 minutes or until the pork turns opaque. Stir in the rice noodles and mix thoroughly.

2 In a bowl, mix together the fish sauce, sugar, lime juice, soy sauce and tomato sauce. Add sauce mixture to the wok, stirring well. Stir-fry for 5 minutes. Mix in the bean sprouts and prawns (shrimps) and stir-fry for a further 5 minutes or until the bean sprouts are tender. Season with black pepper.

3 Transfer to a serving dish. Sprinkle over the peanuts and coriander (cilantro), then serve with the lime wedges.

NUTRITIONAL VALUE PER SERVE	FAT **10.6** G	CARBOHYDRATE **7.1** G	PROTEIN **8** G